STOP

OVERTHINKING

ATTACKING
THE MINDSET OF
SELF DOUBT

Christopher Faulk

TABLE OF CONTENTS

INTRODUCTION

"Try not to squander life in questions and fears; spend yourself on the work before you, all around guaranteed that the correct exhibition of this current hour's obligations will be the best groundwork for the hours and ages that will follow it."

— Ralph Waldo Emerson.

There's a sneaking power that can deny us happiness, certainty, and expectation, sending us spiraling from a confident perspective to one of stress, reluctance, and vulnerability. We peruse and hear a ton about dread and how to battle it and use it for our potential benefit. We regularly don't speak much about the question. It merits starting up the discussion on this malevolent adversary, generally because it's the mysterious fight we all battle — and large numbers of us are (unexpectedly) miserable of opening up about specific issues.

As indicated by Merriam-Webster, dread is "a disagreeable regularly compelling feeling brought about by expectation or attention to risk."

Uncertainty is "to raise doubt about the reality of to be unsure." It is likewise to show an absence of certainty.

Not too far off, we've recognized the differentiation — dread is inwardly based and can overwhelm our intellectual capacities simply by what it means for our active life. Uncertainty is simply the sign of awareness, vulnerability, and serious addressing of reality — the total of what when we'd be best left to take and acknowledge existence as far as we might be concerned to be.

A specific measure of addressing is essential to living a smart, knowing life. We all ought to do this. This article from Harvard Business Review guarantees us of the significance of this scrutinizing:

> *"All sound individuals have an internal stream of contemplations and sentiments that incorporate analysis, uncertainty, and dread. That is only our personalities doing the work they were intended to do: attempting to expect and tackle issues and evade possible entanglements."*
> ### Source: HBR

Regarding the question, it's a matter of perceiving the almost negligible difference between following the Socratic strategy and taking it to the limit. As Susan David and Christina Congleton call attention to, it's a matter of passionate nimbleness:

> *"The initial phase in creating enthusiastic skill is to see when your contemplations and emotions have snared you. That isn't easy to do, yet there are sure indications. One is that your reasoning gets inflexible and dreary. Another is that the story your psyche is telling appears to be old, similar to a rerun of some experience."*
> ### Source: HBR

We can be riding high sincerely and intellectually, accepting we're going the correct way with our motivation and dreams. At that point, out of nowhere, overthinking, an excessive amount of self-doubting prompts a question. Those enormous dreams and objectives appear to be far away. The daily routine we need to experience almost feels like, to a lesser extent, a conviction and considerably more of a question mark.

It's insane how much uncertainty can saturate our lives and lead us to scrutinize individuals, dreams, and reasons we have faith in.

"You don't get to snapshots of a discovery by tolerating disappointment at face esteem, accepting your self-questions to be exact, and stopping by and large."

— Vic Johnson.

HOW DOUBTING YOURSELF HOLD YOU STUCK? (AND HOW TO OVERCOME IT)

How Self-Doubt Keeps You Stuck - How about we picture this:

Your manager has allowed you a significant assignment since he thinks you are the most appropriate individual in the room. However, rather than accepting it as an acknowledgment of your work execution, you begin to freeze.

You alarm about whether you can do extraordinary work. You stress that neglecting to perform well will turn into a significant joke at work. You invest energy worrying about every choice you make and picture how things may turn out badly.

It's not astounding that dread will, at that point, assume a significant part in your little show. It drives you toward hesitation. You defer your work and feel unmotivated.

Toward the finish of the story, you hand in your work at the last possible moment, and it's not difficult to figure that you will have the sensation of "I can show improvement over this."

What causes self-question? How about we discover!

- Past Experience and Mistakes
- Youth Upbringing
- Examinations With Others
- New Challenges
- Dread of Failure/Fear of Success
- For what reason is certainty so significant?

Certainty is putting stock in yourself, feeling good in your actual self, realizing you have worth. Knowing that you are confident, individuals trust you, confidence is alluring, brings achievement, interfaces well with others, and for the most part, feels more joyful.

No one but you can say you're not sure. What reasons do you have preventing you from your certainty?

Step by step instructions to acquire certainty and look after it

1. Have positive brain chat and accept you're a decent individual
2. Learn to like, regard, and love yourself
3. Be social
4. Go outside of your conventional range of familiarity and have a go
5. Remain objective orientated and be glad for your accomplishments
6. Accept praises
7. Do things your great at
8. Consider yourself and know you're a decent individual
9. Spoil yourself
10. Present clean yourself with clean thoughts
11. Accept you and others are not perfect. You commit errors; however, acknowledge obligation
12. Be glad and realize you merit it
13. Accept what your identity is
14. Do things you appreciate
15. Don't put things off
16. Have appreciation
17. Be a caring individual
18. Look forward to life and what's to come
19. Feel you are in charge and have the ability to change things
20. Look for answers for difficulties and approaches to make progress
21. Encourage individuals around you and regard their perspectives
22. Respect your perspectives and defend yourself self-assuredly

CHAPTER 1

WHY WE DOUBT OURSELVES

You look sure. You have the degrees. You have the experience. You're carrying on with an extraordinary life. Anyway, for what reason do you question yourself?

Indeed, there are a variety of reasons why self-question appears in your life. Some may even appear to be substantial; others not really. Regardless, you will not have a possibility of defeating these self-questions, assuming you don't recognize them and build up an arrangement for conquering them. The present article is about the initial segment.

We should begin by taking a gander at eight common reasons why individuals, particularly ladies, question themselves.

1. We Don't Have The Know-How.

Self-uncertainty can be brought about by not having a universal knowledge of a task, an undertaking, or a field. Hopefully, we will know everything, except the odds are that won't occur—the outcome in question. You might be contemplating various situations that you don't feel arranged for, or you're pondering everyone you know who you think would be vastly improved qualified. (Hi, Imposter Syndrome.)

The thing to recollect is that It's typical to question yourself. What makes a difference more is your main thing about it. Furthermore, here's the significant point I'm making. Everybody questions their abilities and skill sooner or later in their life. A few groups are better at concealing those questions and doing it at any rate than others. They realize that how generally will be terrified and going ahead at any rate.

2. We Don't Know What To Expect.

Another integral justification of self-uncertainty to crawl up is dread of the obscure. At the point when you're meeting a renewed individual or taking a new position, you can't in any way, shape, or form have a deep understanding of it. There are a ton of questions, and that can make you awkward or even unfortunate. Furthermore, that dread at that point transforms into self-question. If you don't figure you can do it and don't put yourself out there, you don't need to confront those questions.

In any case, that is an unacceptable quality of life your life.

There is no viable method to know all that will occur on a task, with a venture, or in a relationship. Indeed, we can plan. However, there will consistently be questions. The key is to figure out how to say yes at any rate and sort it out as you come – ask, get savvy counsel, take a gander at all the reasons you should say yes.

3. Our Past Catches Up With Us

We should all had ideal lives without any issues or issues. However, that is simply not the situation. We as a whole accompany our set of experiences and our stuff. Furthermore, a portion of those past encounters makes us question ourselves and our capacities. Possibly it's a bombed relationship that makes us believe we're not ready to deal with a drawn-out responsibility like marriage. Possibly it's an occurrence with a chief or collaborator in a past work that makes us reluctant to go for the advancement Or, on the other hand, possibly it's something unique.

Every one of us has a past, and that previous leaves scars. Some are more profound than others, yet they would all be able to subvert your self-assurance and lead to self-question. Understanding the past is the initial move towards conquering that question and your history with all its stuff.

4. We've Been Told We Can't Do This.

We're social animals, raised in a social climate. We as a whole have families that can look altogether different. Be that as it may, since the beginning, we've figured out how to tune in to what people around us need to say. Specifically, we've focused on our folks, parent figures, guides, educators, and individuals of power. We've figured out how to hear them out and regard their recommendation more often than not.

As it's simply characteristic of questioning yourself and your choices when one of those individuals you admire reveals to you that you can't do it. Once in a while, the council is sound. Some of the time, it's self-serving. The key is to get familiar with the distinction and understand that growing up includes attempting things in any event when your "older folks" preach against it. Since actually, they aren't in every case right.

There are things in your central core that God simply murmured to you. Everybody will not get that. They may cherish and often think about you. However, everybody will not generally concur with you. Piously continue to push ahead.

5. We Are Fearful

In some cases, you're outright terrified. You're apprehensive about the obscure, you're reluctant to wreck, and you're hesitant to discover that you're not sufficient. Dread is a solid inspiration, and for this situation, dread causes self-question and persuades in real life. It leaves you speechless.

That implies you don't go after your fantasy position, you don't go out and get that degree, you don't place your name in the cap for the advancement, and you don't converse with your charming neighbor. Inspired by a paranoid fear of being let down. In any case, learn to expect the unexpected. When we let that dread standard us, we lose any opportunity we had for positive change. Isn't it worth accomplishing something notwithstanding the dread on the off chance that you get a chance of getting what you need?

6. We Lack Self-Worth

We previously discussed how self-question is an absence of trust in our capacity to complete something. It's likewise firmly identified with a lack of self-esteem. The two typically go connected at the hip. We don't believe we're sufficient, and we don't think we have the stuff – absence of self-esteem and lack of certainty. The outcome is a twofold portion of self-question.

Fortunately, as you work on disposing of self-question, your self-esteem will go up and the other way around. Also, that self-esteem will assist you with disposing of self-question. It's a self-pushing cycle. You should simply get the ball moving. To help you with doing that, recall that you are God's absolute favorite. Your worth is more prominent than diamonds, gems, or rubies. Furthermore, there is nor never will be another lady like you – you're a magnum opus.

7. We Don't Think We're Good Enough Yet.

Another enormous issue that causes self-question is believing that we don't know enough yet or haven't encountered enough for an assignment, a task, or a position. That is ordinary. Odds are the point at which you accept another position or have a go at something new, and you may not be as great at it as you'd prefer to be from the outset. That is because you haven't attempted it yet, and you do not have the experience.

It's likewise ordinary to question you can do it. The significant part is to attempt things, at any rate, get some insight added to your repertoire, and improve at what you're doing. Recall the initial not many weeks at your most recent work. The odds are that it was complex and overpowering and that you didn't have the foggiest idea how to do a large portion of the stuff you were out of nowhere answerable for. Be that as it may, you endured those upsetting initial not many weeks in any case. You improved at your particular employment, and ultimately, it got normal – something you could do in your rest. The equivalent goes for figuring out how to drive a vehicle or your number one side interest. It requires some investment, and it's alright to do things sometime before you know it all there is to know, which, incidentally, is preposterous in any case, regardless of how well you plan.

The objective isn't flawlessness – it's finished. Give yourself some beauty and do all that can be expected in the most brilliant manner that you can.

8. We're More Comfortable Where We're At Right Now

This is an intense one. In any case, it's generally very typical – getting too agreeable in your normal range of familiarity.

How about we return to the new position model. Indeed, initially, it was challenging and testing. There was a lot of you didn't have a clue and a ton you needed to sort out. Presently, however, that equivalent occupation has gotten comfortable and surprisingly standard. It's genuinely straightforward, and you realize what to do. You're open to doing what you're doing, and that might be what's holding you back from applying for that advancement, blaming self-question for keeping you agreeable.

In any case, listen to this. You have a decision to make. Will you stay agreeable where you're currently, or would you say you are prepared to get somewhat awkward, face your feelings of trepidation and challenge the obscure? However decent as it could be to remain agreeable, it'll get exhausting in the long run. What's more, recall, dreams don't work out in a safe place. Each one of those endowments, objectives, and plans you need to expect you to get awkward if you need to get things going.

Are these the only reasons why individuals may question themselves? Not. We each come from various foundations and have carried on with altogether different lives. Thus, we've created self-question for multiple reasons. The ones I've recorded here are, nonetheless, a portion of the more normal ones. And keeping in mind that they may not portray you and your conditions impeccably, they should give you a smart thought of where your self-question is coming from. What's more, with that data, you can begin to run after quieting that self-uncertainty and tuning in to your confident voice.

CHAPTER 2

WHERE DOES SELF-QUESTION COME FROM?

Like all propensities, self-uncertainty can emerge out of a wide assortment of sources. Furthermore, indeed, no two individuals' battles with self-question are similar.

For instance, for one individual, self-uncertainty may have begun in adolescence, maybe because of how they were raised. Then again, self-uncertainty can become an issue later in adulthood in light of sudden emergencies or stressors like separation or occupation misfortune.

Also, the components that caused your self-question, in any case, are not generally the very ones that are keeping it up now. Maybe harassing as a kid caused your propensity for self-question at first. Yet, as a grown-up, your psychological propensity for asking others for consolation is the thing that's looking after it.

There are a couple of primary reasons for self-question that I as often as possible find in my work as a therapist:

3 Common Causes of Self-question

While it's essential to recognize that many, numerous things can both reason and keep up the propensity for self-question, three causes appear again and again in my work as an advisor:

1. Narcissistic guardians. It's regularly said that we will, in general, similar recurrent missteps as our folks. In any case, it's similarly as regular that we're so frightened by rehashing our folks' errors that we swing to the next outrageous. Frequently, offspring of narcissistic guardians' are so terrified of being narcissistic that they go to the following absurd and decline to give themselves any commendation, credit, or congrats.
2. The Drill Sergeant Theory of Motivation. From early on, numerous kids discover that the ideal approach to persuade yourself is to "get extreme" with yourself. Like the cliché, the military trainer is reviling his volunteers—since that will "make men out of the"— youngsters figure out how to be excessively condemning of themselves as an inspiration methodology. They frequently build up a dread that they'll become "languid and delicate" without consistent self-analysis and brutality and will not have the option to accomplish any longer.
3. Learned yielding. Numerous youngsters, lamentably, are raised by sincerely immature grown-ups who don't have reliable methods of having a positive outlook on themselves. Subsequently, these grown-ups frequently recognition and award their youngsters with consideration at whatever point they go to them for consolation. This cycle makes a hero complex in guardians and unfortunate reliance in kids when taken to a limit. Since the youngsters discover that they can get quick help from tension by asking their folks for consolation, they never figure out how to deal with their nervousness and settle on choices notwithstanding vulnerability.

Before we proceed onward to taking a gander at the various kinds of self-question, it's essential to explain a significant inquiry:

What's simply the contrast between solid and unfortunate uncertainty?

Solid self-question versus undesirable self-question

The capacity to question ourselves can be something worth being thankful for. Without it, we'd become excessively sure and wind up settling on a wide range of awful choices and undesirable decisions.

While there's no highly contrasting differentiation among solid and unfortunate self-question, here are a couple of general standards to remember:

- If self-question is forever your first response, it's likely unfortunate.
- If self-question appears in numerous or all parts of your life, it's most likely unfortunate.
- If self-question is constant or "tacky" and you struggle overseeing it or getting your consideration off it, it's presumably unfortunate.
- If you regularly lament choices you made on account of your self-question, it's likely undesirable.
- If your self-question hinders significant connections in your day-to-day existence, it's most likely undesirable.
- If self-question significantly affects your capacity to center and manage your job competently, it's most likely undesirable.

So, utilize sound judgment to assess whether self-question is an undesirable propensity in your life. What's more, if all else fails, you can generally accept that it's somewhat unfortunate, attempt to improve it, and see what occurs. On the off chance that your life improves, that would propose your self-question was unfortunate and conceivably that you could profit considerably more from chipping away at it.

What Are simply the Different Types question?

As an adviser, as far as I can say, self-question will, in general, take three essential structures.

Faker condition

Faker condition is the silly dread of being a misrepresentation or not meriting your achievements.

For instance, regardless of how far you move up the company pecking order, you continually feel like you're not as great as your friends and that you're just one mix-up away from being uncovered and embarrassed. Faker disorder is a type of self-question since the propensity produces it for questioning your achievements and capacities.

If you continually question yourself, for what reason would you accept that you're deserving of what you've accomplished?

Self-Harm

In its most miniature complex structure, self-harm is the inclination to sabotage your objectives and qualities. For instance, in the wake of working effectively adhering to your new eating regimen program for a very long time, you gorge on shoddy nourishment three evenings in succession.

When you constantly self-damage yourself, you make yourself an obvious objective for self-analysis and uncertainty.

Uncertainty

Uncertainty is the point at which you reliably battle to settle on even little choices inspired by a paranoid fear of settling on some unacceptable choice and whatever outcomes may result.

When you settle on a café for supper, at that point, question the choice and stress over likely negative results, you produce an eruption of tension. At that point, to rapidly reduce that nervousness, you concede the option to another person, which calms you of the result's duty and diminishes your tension.

Shockingly, over the long haul, hesitation dissolves your confidence and certainty and makes your propensity for self-question considerably more grounded.

Signs that you battle with self-question

What follows are some typical signs or markers that self-question is an issue in your life:

- Difficulty taking commendations. On the off chance that you reliably get on edge or embarrassed at whatever point somebody praises you, it very well may be an indication that you don't esteem yourself enough because of constant self-question. Praises can at times be awkward for anybody. If you consistently battle to take praises and, as often as possible, dodge circumstances where you may be commended, this could be an indication of an issue with self-question.

- Reassurance-chasing. A constant example of requesting consolation when you're disturbed or struggling to settle on choices is habitually an indication of self-question issues. At the point when you question your capacities, it usually creates uneasiness. The fastest method to reduce tension is frequently to request that others choose or disclose to you things are OK. The issue is, this shows your psyche that your judgment isn't reliable, and over the long haul, this just increases your propensity for self-question.

- Low confidence. However, numerous things can prompt low confidence by a long shot; quite possibly, the most widely recognized is self-question. At the point when you consistently uncertain and second-surmise your own choices and inclinations, maybe you had someone else pursuing you around the entire day disclosing to you how imbecilic and dishonest you are. Whether you realized it wasn't accurate, the consistent uncertainty and analysis would begin to wear on you inwardly. Furthermore, it would start to affect your whole personality and ability to be self-aware in the long run.

- Difficulty giving yourself credit. Like struggling to tolerate praises, on the off chance that you routinely battle to give yourself kudos for a job done the right way or essentially accomplishing something pleasant, it very well may be an indication of self-question battles. At the point when the propensity for self-question gains out of power, it tends to "press-out" some other reactions, and uncertainty turns into your default method of deciphering anything you do or accomplish.

- Feeling like you're rarely sufficient. Some, this ought to be self-evident, yet on the off chance that you reliably feel awful about yourself and reliably question your capacities and accomplishments, perhaps there's a connection there. The Difficulty is, self-question—in the same way as other propensities—can turn out to be so programmed and instilled as to be practically undetectable. Be that as it may, if questioning yourself turns out to be just the water you swim in, it isn't easy to envision how you could expect to have a positive outlook on yourself.

CHAPTER 3

SELF-DOUBT DESTROYS THE HEART, MIND, BODY, AND SOUL

The vast majority of us have encountered self-question sooner or later in our lives. How we manage it, how we adapt to it, implies the distinction between battling persistently with self-uncertainty and releasing it decently fast. If we experience constant self-question, we may ask: Why does every other person appear to do so well when I battle to such an extent?

Sound Self-question

Some degree of self-question in specific circumstances can be sound. Self-question exists, all things considered, to assist us with remembering we're not in every case right. With self-question, we question and challenge ourselves as we reflect internally. With some self-question, we have modesty and can relate better to other people.

Unfortunate Self-question

In any case, in a general public that qualities the exceptional, it's way more normal for self-uncertainty to turn into a persistent state. When it does, we regularly start to "hinder us" and struggle to see beneficial things about ourselves. This is an undesirable self-question.

When we can't see our excellent characteristics, it's hard to look for inspiration. We may accept that we'll never accomplish our objectives, that we don't have the ability, are not deserving of our position or accomplice. Minor disappointments start to be evidence of our dishonor. Undesirable self-uncertainty can measure up to an eager parasite that devours increasingly more of you, benefiting from your confidence, self-esteem, and self-adequacy.

The Inner Critic

There are mental components self-cynics use to maintain and sustain their undesirable disposition toward themselves.

"I can't"— The Self-satisfying Prophecy.

How we address ourselves more than once after some time, in the end, frames grooves in our neural pathways. If we reveal to ourselves some "I'm a failure," "I'm unequipped for doing.

"I'm terrible"—Lack of Self-kindness

By keeping your sense from getting accomplishment, you're likewise adding to a more significant issue identified with an absence of self-consideration. As a rule, we are very steady and sustaining companions out of luck; we will be a lot harsher with ourselves in general. Studies give that the absence of self-grace can anticipate self-question. Kinder people will, in general, acknowledge, as opposed to denying, their lacks and better urge themselves to improve. Since those with high self-question have a more critical requirement for endorsement from others, they stress disappointments and negative assessments and are harsher in their self-decisions. This prompts an inclination toward seclusion.

Self-question—Risk Factor for Depression

Various investigations have discovered an association between consistent self-question and mental issues, for example, disposition swings, lower confidence, tension, and misery. Large numbers of the side effects used to determine sorrow relate to having examples of self-question. At the point when self-question causes a misfortune in inspiration or fixation, or sensations of uncertainty, blame, disgrace, or uselessness, this is when sadness can set in.

Melancholy may achieve cynicism in the future, evasion of obligation, social disconnection, and uneasiness or fears. Consequently, don't make light of sorrow! If there's a chance you're discouraged, don't question that also!

Self-question is just unsafe when it is ongoing. So how would you know the distinction?

Ongoing self-skeptics are more centered around not fizzling than they are on the main job. They think it's hard to make the most of their work since they are loaded up uneasily as they approach certain errands.

There are numerous results of self-question, yet here are three that researchers have found could be an indication that you are disrupting your prosperity:

- Self-incapacitating happens when we intentionally subvert our exhibition in some assignment or try, consequently improving the probability of disappointment trying to darken the justification disappointment. For instance, if I am tormented with self-question and become inebriated before my presentation and make an awful showing, I would now be able to fault the liquor. This causes me to feel better than confronting how I may have fizzled due to my deficiencies.
- Impostor wonder likewise alluded to as "impostor disorder," happens when a successful individual is unequipped for crediting their accomplishments to their ability or abilities and has determined sensations of being a fake. Any achievement they have is excused as excellent fortune or their capacity to trick others that they are more intelligent and capable than they are. Dissimilar to the self-handicapper who darkens the justification disappointment, individuals with the impostor marvel dark the justification achievement.
- Procrastination permits us to defer an assignment when we realize our exhibition will be socially assessed. As individuals, we are more engaged and worried about how our

presentation will be decided than with the actual exhibition's prosperity. If we are stressed over how we will 'look' before others, we may put off the errand (even inconclusively) to ensure our self-esteem sensations.

CHAPTER 4

WHAT SELF-DOUBT MEANS FOR YOUR RELATIONSHIP

Have you at any point arrived at the cut-off of an association, and upon reflection, acknowledged how huge a job your low confidence played in the separation? Your faith in yourself and the certainty it motivates you to have an urgent influence in making your' relationship material'.

An absence of confidence and having confidence in yourself can cause numerous possible issues in your relationship. If your accomplice has these characteristics, yet you don't, there will be an awkwardness in the relationship. Such connections are difficult to support and frequently end in a split.

Through some genuine reflection, you can discover the seeds of self-question in your psyche and address them straightforwardly. If you don't, this is how self-uncertainty will deal with your relationship:

1. You become mutually dependent

When you feel that the solitary way you can characterize yourself is through your accomplice because of their self-assuredness, you will distance your identity. You become a sad remnant of your previous self as you get gobbled up in the relationship.

Before long, you will not feel particular about any choice you need to make, and you'll re-think yourself at whatever point you find the opportunity. You'll constantly look for your accomplice's endorsement for pretty much anything. It can arrive where you can't choose what tone to paint a room without first counseling your accomplice.

Honestly, that is not counseling; it's requesting authorization and giving your accomplice unlimited oversight over you. The vast majority don't care for having somebody who is so vigorously reliant on them, and you wind up driving your accomplice away. It probably won't occur that way, and it's conceivable your accomplice can delight in oppressing you and being in finished control.

2. You feel expanded degrees of nervousness.

At the point when you question yourself, you begin to address whether you even have the right to be seeing someone. You stress that your accomplice is excessively useful for you, and it might be said, you're sitting tight for them to acknowledge it and leave you. These sentiments can prompt sensations of excessive nervousness in individuals with low confidence.

You replay each discussion you've had with your accomplice, searching for the subtext or covered up importance in each sentence they utter when it simply isn't there.

The nervousness deteriorates when you consider what you said and can't help thinking about how your accomplice deciphered it. Your accomplice isn't doing a posthumous on the discussion, and they've effectively proceeded onward to something different.

Tension can be devastating and debilitating, and it can assume control over your life. It is an envious fancy woman that requests all your consideration constantly, and it will shove your accomplice to the aside to set aside more space for itself in your brain.

Your accomplice will detect your detachedness and start to address whether you're 'the one.' Other cozy associations with companions, family, and partners will begin to piece, also.

3. You become the cause of all your problems.

Numerous individuals have low confidence and uncertainty in all their choices due to an occasion before they have not prepared. It is generally identified with a deficiency of trust in an individual near or an untidy cut-off to an association. Without managing these issues, you are continually trusting that set of experiences will rehash the same thing.

At this stage, the only hindrance confronting you in your relationship is you. Oneself attacking conduct and a definitive end of the relationship would not occur, yet for the way that you don't have faith in yourself.

Over the long haul, low confidence gets harmful in a relationship, and your questions and fears cloud your psyche. You can't see the relationship for what it is because you're shading it with your past encounters. This prompts you to avoid your accomplice as much as possible and destroying the relationship without help from anyone else.

4. Antagonism burns through you

Your emotions toward yourself pervade each circumstance or relationship you're in, and it's simple for cynicism to dominate. It renders you unfit to see the bright side of anything, and you become the misanthrope, who is somebody individuals effectively dodge. Who needs to associate with somebody who cuts the temperament down any place they go?

These sensations of persevering pessimism can prompt the beginning of a burdensome scene, which can put a strain on the relationship if your accomplice isn't understanding. There's as yet a shame encompassing psychological wellness conditions, and being determined to have one may change how your accomplice sees you.

In case you don't do the fundamental self-reflection, you will not get what your cynicism is the meaning for your relationship until it's past the point of no return. Request that yourself what's going on cause you to feel along these lines and what you need to do. Figure out how to function through what's befalling you and your relationship by seeing a guide or specialist for help.

5. Outrage overpowers you

You realize that what you're doing will demolish your relationship. However, you can't stop yourself. Your dissatisfaction levels assemble, and gradually moving indignation grabs hold of you. Who are you furious with? The primary individual you're frantic at is yourself, yet it's not in every case simple to concede that.

Thus, you check out for individuals to criticize for what you're feeling. It should be your ex who undermined you, or it's your dad since you figure he didn't cherish you enough. It's that educator from secondary school who disclosed to you that you wouldn't add up to much throughout everyday life. And afterward, you center your resentment nearer to home, concluding that the individual to blame is your accomplice.

You become inclined to furious upheavals, making statements you neither feel nor mean. The hurt you cause your accomplice will make them question the intelligence of remaining in a relationship with you.

6. You set yourself last.

At the point when you don't have confidence and your life is overwhelmed without anyone else question, you start to put every other person and their requirements in front of you. You grumble about it like a casualty and saint all folded into one, weeping over how benevolent you are agreeable to other people. Hatred toward your accomplice begins rotting in your brain.

Also, that is the thing that you are: sacrificial, as in being without an ability to be self-aware. You feel so little worth as an individual that you view yourself as contemptible of adoration and joy. So centered are you around doing the 'best thing' by putting every other person first to annihilate yourself all the while.

7. Modify your certainty

On the off chance that you know you're liable for these practices, don't sit and overanalyze them, rebuffing yourself accordingly. Begin dealing with an arrangement to improve your confidence and lessen the sensations of self-question that frequent you wherever you go. Everything isn't lost, and there is a ton you can do to cure the circumstance.

Open up to your accomplice about your battles and request their help. Reveal to them that you probably won't be challenging to cherish on occasion, yet you're remaking yourself for your excellent and the relationship's advantage.

CHAPTER 5

THE 21-DAY CHALLENGE ON REGAINING SELF-CONFIDENCE

Building solid certainty and disposing of self-question doesn't happen.

I have a fantastic technique that has helped me develop trust and conquer self-doubt.

I jot down notes, and it's as easy as it sounds.

I will recognize what makes me fearful by writing down items that make me doubt myself and reviewing them weekly. This helps me develop opportunities to better myself.

I begin to love myself more and reflect on what I have rather than what I lack as I write down stuff about which I am thankful.

I've already stopped comparing myself to someone, and looking at what I've posted reminds me that I'm content with my own life.

This is my 21-day strategy for regaining self-confidence, and it's something you can try as well!

Days 1 to 7: Every day, write three things you're grateful for.

When you look back on them at the end of the week, you'll see that the more you post, the more you'll notice that many things will make you smile.

HOW SELF-DOUBT KEEPS YOU STUCK (AND HOW TO OVERCOME IT)

on the off-chance **days 8 to 14**: Write Times You Feel Unsure About Yourself and Reasons Behind Them

Toward the week's end, you ought to have the option to distinguish your most significant feelings of dread and minutes that cause you to feel focused.

During the survey cycle, you can begin to consider approaches to take care of your issues. It tends to be "zeroing in additional on myself" or things you think you need to enhance.

Days 15 to 21: Write Steps You've Taken and How You Feel

Regardless of how you've dealt with conquered self-question, record them and perceive yourself!

We as a whole need inspiration alongside the way, and regardless of how little the means you have taken, they show that you are one bit nearer to what you need to accomplish!

Doing so propels you. However, it assists you in keeping focused on your advancement.

Last Thoughts

It's normal and typical to question ourselves. However, it would be beneficial if you realized that remaining stuck and freezing for a long time will not benefit you in any way.

Attempt to escape the circle straightaway and invest energy developing yourself. Self-question doesn't need to keep you down.

CHAPTER 6

LET GO OF SELF-DOUBT: A NEW MINDSET

At the point when you question, your brain accepts what you feel and think. Afterward, your psyche is customized to accept that your fantasies are impossible; however, disappointment, normally, inspires you to invest more effort. Hence, you succeed the following time you endeavor to arrive at your fantasies. Questions make you divert your destinations. This can make you go to some unacceptable way or even to surrender totally.

When you fizzle, you become more grounded, and you make it one bit nearer to your objectives. On the off chance that you continue to push ahead, you will prevail at arriving at the prize in the end. Visionaries are not individuals who have disturbing thoughts; however, individuals who will remain with their views during the hour of disappointments. Questions keep us away from arriving at our maximum capacity. Disappointment is only a venturing stone. Without it, we can't learn. It's a piece of the cycle.

Disappointment, ordinarily, propels you to invest more effort with the goal that you succeed the following time you endeavor to arrive at your fantasies. Uncertainty can derail from your targets because, as referenced prior, it comes right on time, before acting. Embrace disappointments as they will possibly improve you on the off chance that you gain from them. Your capacities can improve, while disappointment is only an occasion. Try not to allow it to enhance the haziness of self-question. The two of them cooperate and attempt to take your fantasies from you. Try not to allow that to occur. Uncertainty executes a more significant number of dreams than disappointment at any point will.

"Assuming you hear a voice inside you say you can't paint, by all methods paint, and that voice will be hushed."

— Vincent van Gogh.

Acting quickly is simply the initial step to defeat the question. To assemble long-haul certainty, you need to build up another attitude. Here's the secret.

1. Embrace the distress of strangeness. At the point when you accomplish something interestingly, it feels odd. Indeed, even the most experienced specialists experience the ill effects of the "impostor disorder."

It takes more than one movement for you to turn into the part. Practicing is the thing that transforms an entertainer into a critical one. You should turn into the character before others begin to look all starry-eyed at it.

Disregard being criticized. Fruitful individuals are accustomed to having a greater number of pundits than fans. The more remarkable your craft, the more profound you'll interface for specific individuals, the more others will dismiss you. As Winston Churchill said: "You have adversaries? Great. That implies you've gone to bat for something, at some point in your life."

Embrace a learning mind.

Receive the being uninformed mentality. I'm not saying bring down your bar. Yet, try not to set it too high that it can scare you. Change your bar. Intend to be the incredible amateurs. Try not to attempt to beat prepared tennis players when you are simply beginning.

Quietness, your inward pundit.

Compulsiveness is the adversary of progress. Quiet is overthinking. Each time you question yourself, simply say 'question' to get mindful of what's happening. Furthermore, proceed onward. Try not to get trapped in self-question. That Feeling can show up startlingly. It happens to me as well. In any case, that doesn't mean uncertainty merits room in your brain. Quietness, your internal pundit. Account for the voice you had always wanted.

You needn't bother with an arrangement B.

My companion Jack was energetic around one thought. He had everything about out. However, when I asked him for what valid reason he hadn't dispatched at this point, he began sharing different thoughts he had. They appeared to be vaguer than the one that made him tick.

"I need choices." — He advised me. That is the reason he hasn't dispatched at this point. Having choices is something contrary to the center.

Achievement requires centering your energy. Having a Plan B weakens your responsibility when you are in the stream. There's consistently an ideal opportunity to change as you go. As John Lennon said: "Life is the thing that occurs while you are occupied with making different arrangements." Pivot and repeat as a characteristic movement expanding on experience as opposed to on expectation.

Progress isn't direct.

When I chose to up my trekking game, it felt smooth to speed up and cycle longer distances. Extending my objectives was empowering and fulfilling. Consistently I was arriving at another high. Until one day, I didn't gain any headway. Furthermore, the week from that point onward, my exhibition diminished. I felt disappointed. It took me mindfulness and preparing to conquer that level.

Reaching a stopping point is a fundamental piece of progress. When things get hard, this is because you are prepared for the following stretch. If you don't feel an obstruction, you are not propelling yourself excessively hard.

Become hopelessly enamored with your actual self.

"In a general public that benefits from your self-question, loving yourself is a defiant demonstration."

— Anonymous.

Adoring yourself is not gullible. If you don't turn into your dearest companion, who else will? On the off chance that you don't pass on trust in what you do, don't anticipate that others should confide in you. As C.S. Lewis said: "We are what we accept we are."

At the point when you embrace your actual personality, there's no space for self-question.

The sad remnant of self-uncertainty may show up startlingly. It's dependent upon you to move from dimness to light.

How does self-question influence you? Which of these experiences and tips will you incorporate?

CHAPTER 7

DEFEATING FEAR OF FAILURE

Confronting Your Fear of Moving Forward

Have you ever been so terrified of something? Coming up short at something that you chose not to attempt by any means? Or then again, has a dread of disappointment implied that, subliminally, you subverted your endeavors to maintain a strategic distance from the chance of a more significant blow?

A significant number of us have likely encountered this at some time. The dread of coming up short can be immobilizing – it can make us sit idle, and consequently, pushing forward is not a bright idea.

Whatever the case might be, if we approve it, dread to stop our forward progress throughout everyday life, we're probably going to pass up on some extraordinary chances en route.

In this article, we'll inspect the dread of disappointment: what it implies, what causes it, and how to conquer it to appreciate genuine progress in work and life.

Defeat your feelings of trepidation and push ahead to accomplish your objectives!

Reasons for Fear of Failure

To discover the reasons inspired by a paranoid fear of disappointment, we first need to get what "disappointment" really implies.

We have various meanings of disappointment just because we have multiple benchmarks, qualities, and conviction frameworks. An inability to one individual may essentially be an extraordinary learning experience for another person.

A considerable lot of us fear falling flat, probably a portion of the time. In any case, the dread of disappointment (likewise called "atychiphobia") is the point at which we permit that dread to prevent us from doing the things that can push us ahead to accomplish our objectives.

Dread of disappointment can be connected to numerous causes. For example, having primary or unsupportive guardians is a reason for specific individuals. Since they were regularly subverted or embarrassed in adolescence, they convey those negative emotions into adulthood.

Encountering a horrible accident eventually in your life can likewise be a reason. For instance, say that you gave a significant introduction before an enormous gathering quite a while prior, and you did it inadequately. The experience may have been horrendous to the point that you got scared of coming up short in different things. Also, you convey that dread even now, a long time later.

How You Experience Fear of Failure

You may encounter a few of these manifestations if you have a dread of disappointment:

- A hesitance to attempt new things or engage in testing projects.
- Self-harm – for instance, Procrastination, over-the-top tension, or an inability to finish objectives.
- Low confidence or fearlessness – ordinarily utilizing negative proclamations, for example, "I'll never be sufficient to get that

advancement," or "I'm not shrewd enough to get in that group."

- Perfectionism – An eagerness to attempt just those things that you realize you'll complete consummately and effectively.

The Definition of Failure

It's practically difficult to go through existence without encountering some sort of disappointment. Individuals who do so likely live so mindfully that they go no place. Set forth plainly, and they're not inhabiting all.

Yet, the brilliant thing about disappointment is that it's altogether dependent upon us to conclude what to look like at it.

We can consider the inability to be "the apocalypse" or evidence of exactly how insufficient we are. Or on the other hand, we can view disappointment as the extraordinary learning experience that it frequently is. Each time we come up short at something, we can decide to search for the exercise we're intended to learn. These exercises are vital; they're how we develop and continue to commit that equivalent error once more. Disappointments stop us just if we let them.

It's not difficult to track down influential individuals who have encountered disappointment. For instance:

- Michael Jordan is generally viewed as one of the best basketball players ever. He was cut from his secondary school basketball group since his mentor didn't think he had sufficient expertise.
- Warren Buffet, one of the world's most extravagant and best financial specialists, was dismissed by Harvard University.
- Richard Branson, the proprietor of the Virgin domain, is a secondary school dropout.
-

The majority of us will stagger and fall throughout everyday life. Entryways will get closed forcefully, and we may settle on some terrible choices. In any case, envision if Michael Jordan had abandoned his fantasy to play b-ball when he was cut from that group. Imagine if Richard Branson had tuned in to individuals who revealed to him he'd do nothing beneficial without a secondary school confirmation.

Think about the chances you'll miss if you let your disappointments stop you.

Disappointment can likewise show us things ourselves that we couldn't have ever learned something else. For example, disappointment can assist you with finding how solid an individual you are. Coming up short at something can help you find your most genuine companions or help you track down the startling inspiration to succeed.

Frequently, essential experiences come solely after a disappointment. Tolerating and gaining from those experiences is critical to prevailing throughout everyday life.

How Not to Be Afraid of Failure

Understand that there's consistently a possibility that we'll fall flat in all that we do. Confronting that opportunity, and accepting it, isn't just brave – it additionally gives us a more full, seriously compensating life.

In any scenario, here are a few suggestions. Approaches to decrease the dread of falling flat:

- Analyze every possible result – Many individuals experience the dread of disappointment since they dread the obscure. Eliminate that dread by thinking about the entirety of the expected results of your choice. Our article Decision Trees will show you how to plan potential outcomes outwardly.
- Learn to think all the more emphatically – Positive reasoning is an unbelievably unique approach to assemble fearlessness and kill self-damage. Thought Awareness, Rational Thinking, and Positive Thinking is a new article we've written. An extensive asset for figuring out how to change your musings.
- Look at the direst outcome imaginable – at times, the direct result possible might be lamentable, and it very well might be

objective to fear disappointment. In different cases, in any case, this most pessimistic scenario may not be that terrible, and perceiving this can help.

- Have an alternate course of action – If you're apprehensive about coming up short at something, having a "Plan B" set up can help you feel more certain about pushing ahead.

Instructions to Stop Living in Fear

If you fear disappointment, you may be awkward defining objectives. In any case, objectives assist us with characterizing where we need to go throughout everyday life. Without goals, we have no definite purpose.

Numerous specialists suggest representation as an incredible asset for objective setting. Envisioning how life will be after you've arrived at your objective is an extraordinary spark to keep you pushing ahead.

Be that as it may, the representation may create contrary outcomes in individuals who dread disappointment. Examination shows that individuals who dread disappointment were frequently left in a solid negative mindset in the wake of being approached to envision objectives and objective achievement.

All in all, what would you be able to do?

Start by defining a couple of little objectives. These ought to be objectives that are marginally, yet not overwhelmingly, testing. Consider these objectives "early successes" that are intended to help support your certainty.

For instance, if you've been too reluctant to even think about conversing with the new office head (who can give you the advancement you need), at that point, make that your first objective. Make a point of visiting her office during the day. Following week to present yourself.

Or on the other hand, envision that you've longed to get back to class to get your MBA. However, you're persuaded that you're not keen enough to be acknowledged into business college. Set an objective to converse with a school guide or confirmation official to perceive what's needed for affirmation.

Attempt to make your objectives small strides in transit to a lot more significant objectives. Try not to zero in on the end picture: getting the advancement or graduating with an MBA. Simply center around the following stage: acquainting yourself with the division head and conversing with an affirmations official. That is it.

Making each little stride, in turn, will help fabricate your certainty, keep you pushing ahead, and keep you from getting overpowered with dreams of your last objective.

Caution:

Some of the time, fearing disappointment can be an indication of a more genuine emotional well-being condition. Negative reasoning can cause serious medical issues and, in outrageous cases, passing. While these procedures have appeared to affect decreasing pressure positively, they are for direction, and perusers should accept the counsel of reasonably qualified well-being experts if they have any worries over related diseases or if negative musings are causing massive or determined misery. Well-being experts ought to likewise be counseled before any significant change in diet or levels of activity.

Central issues

A significant number of us are here and there terrified of coming up short, yet we mustn't allow that dread to prevent us from pushing ahead.

Dread of disappointment can have a few causes: from youth occasions to botches we've made in our grown-up lives. Understand that we generally have a decision: we can decide to be apprehensive or decide not to be.

Start by defining little objectives that will help assemble your certainty. Figure out how to investigate and assess all possible results judiciously, create emergency courses of action, and work on reasoning emphatically. By pushing ahead gradually, however consistently, you'll start to conquer your dread.

CHAPTER 8

DISAPPOINTMENT IS THE KEY TO SUCCESS

Perhaps the main faculties most people have is torment. Agony permits us to gain rapidly from our mix-ups. Getting a sharp item, falling over, chancing upon things, dropping something on your foot; the suffering included rapidly permits youngsters to learn not to do these things.

Without the agony, kids would not learn through their disappointments. Without this disappointment, they would not figure out how to succeed.

Moving into adulthood and expert life, disappointment is frequently seen as something negative. Assume a business dispatches another item, attempts another advertising activity, or attempts another client experience on their site. The movement will often have KPIs zeroed in on components like development in deals, a development in benefit, or an expansion in orders.

This is entirely reasonable and characteristic for most organizations. Partners should gauge the achievement and ROI of any activity.

On the off chance that from the start, you don't succeed...

While achievement ought to surely be commended, what can make an organization stand apart isn't exactly how it manages achievement; however, how it manages disappointment.

As individuals and organizations, we're all going to bomb now and then.

No individual or organization is effective at everything, and disappointment can show us an extraordinary arrangement.

Advancement frequently includes facing a challenge, here and there large, in some cases minor. Any danger gets an opportunity of disappointment, so it makes sense that the dread of disappointment represses hazard taking, hindering advancement.

I've run Envoy for more than 20 years, and, in that time, we have had the two victories and disappointments (fortunately, a more significant amount of the previous and less of the last mentioned). We've run many tasks, and each has had its difficulties, victories, and disappointments.

The significant thing is to comprehend the disappointments and gain from them.

I've positively tracked down that the most complex and most essential exercises have consistently come from our disappointments – it's what at last assisted us with getting fruitful.

If you're interested, have a look at it in fruitful business people's set of experiences, you'll frequently see they had numerous disappointments before getting effective. Does anybody recollect the Apple Newton? That was a great disappointment. However, I question whether we'd have iPhones and iPads currently had Apple not dispatched the Newton and realized why it fizzled.

What about the Apple Lisa? This was a massive disappointment for the organization and, at last expense, Steve Jobs his work. Would we currently have the Apple Mac had they not gained from the frustration of the Lisa?

James Dyson created a vast number of his vacuum cleaner models, gaining from everyone preceding concocting a rendition that worked and urged him to be one of the world's best business visionaries.

Gaining from disappointment is significant, taking all things together parts of life and business – from numerous points of view, disappointment is the way to progress.

A/B or multivariate testing is genuinely standard for most online retailers where various designs, messages, invitations to take action, and capacities are tried against each other to see which accomplishes the best outcome.

While it's characteristic to zero in on those tests that accomplished the best outcome, those that achieved the most noticeably terrible are similarly significant or, in some cases, more effective.

A test that changed the shade of the checkout catch to blue expanded the transformation rate by 0.1%, however transforming it to red diminished by 0.5%. You could contend that the fizzled test is the most significant as it features the significance of that button's shade. Fail to understand the situation, and you can significantly diminish your change rate.

Amazon is celebrated for zeroing in on proof-based client experience. Any progressions to their foundation's client experience are entirely tried and simply accessible to everybody once the proof shows the proper outcomes. They never convey changes, just dependent on the assessment of one or a couple of individuals.

Disappointment is the way to progress: Try, at that point, attempt once more.

It's essential to adopt this strategy while executing any plan or change to the client experience. I've seen countless models in the past where a shift in UX depends on one UX creator or the simply interior internet business group.

This can regularly be an error. It's critical to test UX changes either through A/B testing or, for more significant changes, client model testing.

Client model testing is the place where an interactive model is tried with a gathering of clients. This can be an unfathomably important exercise to embrace. You will frequently track down UX territory, or usefulness by all accounts clear to the architects befuddles genuine clients.

We had a genuine illustration of this during a new venture. We built up an online arrangement for an item that is very unpredictable to purchase. We were delighted with this device, and both the customer and the originators felt that the device was straightforward and natural to utilize. All things considered, when the interactive model was placed before clients who didn't have a clue about the item quite well, it immediately turned out to be evident that clients got lost and discovered the instrument hard to utilize.

This disappointment was an unimaginably important exercise and permitted us to return and update the instrument and retest it an excessive amount of better achievement.

The absolute greatest and best organizations on the planet have tried commending disappointments that have come to fruition through suitable danger taking and advancement, just as their victories.

Goodbye broadly has a 'Set out to Try' grant, which is granted to those disappointments that came through the advancement and gave the organization some critical exercises. Delegate and Gamble have a 'Chivalrous Failure' grant that praises representatives or groups who acquired the most understanding from a disappointment.

What is essential among these activities is that they support advancement and hazard taking and acknowledge that disappointments can offer practical exercises that help the association succeed.

Suppose an organization is continually falling flat and doesn't transform those disappointments into progress. In that case, it won't keep going throughout the entire that, yet an organization that fears disappointment and doesn't gain from it is seldom going to be a triumph.

CHAPTER 9

THE MOST EFFECTIVE METHOD TO BEAT SELF-DOUBT AND STOP SELLING YOURSELF SHORT

Self-question is an integral part of the human experience as it ought to be. We don't need to look too far even to consider seeing that too minimal self-uncertainty can be out and out hazardous. However, left unchecked, the dread that powers our uncertainty can drive us to be over mindful and hold us back from making similar moves to help us and serve others. I see very numerous proficient and gifted individuals (especially ladies) undercutting themselves since they dread they don't have the stuff to succeed. Uncertainty sits victorious. Activities go fixed.

We don't get the telephone and settle on the decision. We don't expand the greeting. We don't lift our hand for advancement. We don't say "Enough!". We don't push back, say no, say indeed, proceed onward, make a plunge, or get the pen.

Talking about which, I was devoured by the question when composing a book initially grabbed hold of my creative mind. "Who am I to compose a book?" I contemplated internally. I'd never considered writing, and I completed my schooling in provincial

Australia while never realizing where to put every one of the punctuations. However much placing my thoughts into composition roused me, I felt utterly lacking for the undertaking (also that I had four children under seven at that point!) It was just when my significant other Andrew said, "Why not allow yourself to compose a defective book?" that I chose to dive in. Was it the most exceedingly terrible, most prominent piece of scholarly handwriting the world has at any point seen? Not. However, it's presently out on the planet (in six dialects), and it couldn't have ever been had question made significant decisions.

I speculate that self-doubt has been a significant (and understandable) factor behind why so many of the women and men who've come forward in recent months to call out perpetrators of sexual harassment and assault - from Harvey Weinstein to Matt Lauer - didn't do so earlier. They doubted their voice would be heard. They questioned they'd be taken seriously. Some probably even doubted whether they were partly to blame. Self-doubt has much to answer for.

However, while none of us are invulnerable to self-question (except some chronic narcissists that ring a bell), we as a whole can hold it back from coordinating our choices, proceeding with our quietness, and forming our lives. So how would we exile the uncertainty? We don't. What we do is figure out how to recover the force it has held over us. You can do it in six different ways.

1. Embrace Doubt As Part of Being Human

As you consider the things, you'd most love to accomplish or change in your life at Present, realize that self-question is there to shield you from the embarrassment of crashing and burning. So follow the counsel of Dr. Kristen Neff, self-sympathy master, and "Don't pound yourself for pummeling yourself." Far better than thrashing on your inward pundit is to get to know it, to recognize that it's simply attempting to keep you protected and spare you embarrassment. Accepting self-question as a natural piece of the human experience is vital to recovering the force it has held over you up to this point. You are human. You will ruin. You will question yourself. It's your specialty next that is important. This carries me to the subsequent advance.

2. Uncertainty Your Doubts

Self-questions are only your feelings of dread made show to shield you from misfortune. However, the paradox is that to reword Shakespeare, the question frequently causes you to miss out on what you may have acquired by dreading the endeavor. Your questions are not reality. Or maybe they are dread fuelled stories you make about your identity, the thing you're worth, and what you're equipped for accomplishing. So let me rehash only once again to ensure you got it:

Your questions are not reality.

As a general rule, they're the polar opposite. So the following time, you begin to question yourself, pause for a minute to challenge that idea, to examine your questions! Ask yourself, "Imagine a scenario where the polar opposite was valid?" What on the off chance that you were more than arranged for a more outstanding job. On the off chance that you had everything, it takes to construct that business? If what you needed to say was critical? On the off chance that you were more than gifted/commendable/sharp/(fill-in-the-clear) enough to seek after this objective?

If you question anything about yourself to accomplish what you need or change what you don't, ask your questions.

3. Get down on Your Critic

Frequently we hear our questions transferred through the voice of our' internal pundit.' You know the one... it's continually bringing up your flaws, scrutinizing your value (it's the central offender for the Imposter Syndrome), and encouraging you to avoid any risks. While you can't forever quiet it, you can weaken its force by giving it a name. Doing so assists you with recognizing who you are from the dread and uncertainty you feel. Brainstorm a word the best depicts the frightened piece of you that needs you to live little and stay safe. You may even need to compose a short letter to it to advise if you're done going to allow it to manage everything. "Dear Doubting Deborah, it's time..."

4. Make Your Mission Bigger Than Your Fear

For what reason would you try to shout out and hazard causing trouble or being dismissed? For what reason would you lay your standing on the line? For what reason would you take a risk on that fantasy? Just when you are clear about your huge 'Why,' would you be able to discover the grit expected to venture through your questions and hazard coming up short. You should have the option to track down a reasonable and convincing response to the inquiry, "For what am I able to be bold?" Doing so will help take shape why you should make a move regardless of your questions, realizing that on the off chance that you let them win, you will run the greater danger of one day thinking back and considering, 'Imagine a scenario where I'd had a go at?' Letting self-question sit steering the ship is a specific fire formula for lament and disdain.

5. Assemble A Tribe of Believers

You shape your clan, and your family shapes you. Authority of life is not a performance attempt. At the point when you encircle yourself with individuals who draw out your best and energize your reasoning, you can accomplish more, be more, and give more than you at any point could something else.

Individuals you spend time with will either fuel your self-uncertainty or fuel your certainty. So in case, you're prepared to roll out an improvement or take a risk, ensure you encircle yourself with individuals who will help you stay in real life, notwithstanding your questions. Evade the individuals who will not!

6. Train The Brave. Every day

There is nobody step enchantment shot for conquering self-uncertainty and building self-assurance. We construct trust in increases; by daring to make a move regardless of our qualms. We do this in several ways by using BJ Fogg's exploration at Stanford University, which found that downsizing more extraordinary practices into more modest 'scaled down' activities can make dynamic movements that last. Consider fortitude like a muscle; the more you act with it, the more courageous you become. Be that as it may, you must 'train the courageous' day by day.

The ideal approach to 'train the courageous' is to begin right where you are correct now with whatever issue or opportunity you are confronting and ask yourself, "What might I do well now if I were bold?" Chances are, your questions will be shouting at you to do the exact inverse. Say thanks to them for attempting to ensure you, at that point, reveal to them you're not here to carry on with a protected life; you're here to carry on with the most excellent everyday routine you are equipped for experiencing. At that point, put your hand on your heart, envision your prosperity, take a significant long breath, and afterward, DO IT! As exploration has found and experience has shown me, each time you make a move within sight of your questions, you weaken their power and enhance your own.

When you try to do the very thing you question, you can understand how little you at any point expected to ask yourself, regardless.

CHAPTER 10

CONCLUSION

We all deal with self-doubt. It's not something that's ever actually going to go away, so you've got to figure out how you will reframe it. How are you going to use self-doubt as a tool to motivate you, to make you stay driven, to make sure that, even in those things you're scared of, you approach them with courage? Self-doubt isn't something you should be upset that you have. I go onto arenas where there are 25,000 people in the audience, and I'm backstage, and I have that anxiety, I have that concern. I doubt, 'Am I going to do a good job today?' And I worry about it, too. Everybody has self-doubt. The challenge is, some people think they don't need ever to have it, and some people are using it as a tool to stop moving towards their dreams instead of progressing towards their goals. So here are four big ideas on how to better deal with self-doubt so that you can still go after your dreams.

#1: Reframe confidence.

You have to reframe confidence. A lot of people say, "Brendon, I'm just not confident. I wish I were more confident, and I wish I had more fire; I wish I believed in myself more. I always worry about myself, I never believe in myself, I'm always selling myself short, and I never give myself credit. I just quit." I think what happens for many people is they just never really learned what absolute confidence is. Sometimes the truth is that you can be confident but still have doubts about capabilities- and that makes you real. It makes you a non-egomaniac because only super egomaniacs completely lack self-doubt. And so self-doubt can be OK.

What you have to figure out is, what does confidence mean to you? Instead of worrying so much about the doubt, what's the opposite? What's the other part of that? What does confidence mean to you?

We did the most extensive study that's ever been done on high performers worldwide, and what we learned is, the most successful people in the world approach confidence in this way: they believe in their ability to figure things out. It doesn't mean they don't have self-doubt; they think, "I can figure things out. Give me enough time, energy, resources, mentorship, support, and I can figure anything out." You have to start believing that.

As much as you spend time questioning yourself, you have to think, "Can I remember that I figured out things in the past that I wasn't prepared for?" You've done projects in the past, you've been in situations in the past where you had no idea how to handle it, but you figured it out. Take confidence in that. The next time you're going into a situation, and all you can do is think about yourself freak out; what I want you to do is to remember all of those times where you did overcome the doubts, you did overcome the anxiety, you overcame the lack of skills, the unknowns, and you still pulled it off.

There are more times in your life that you overcame self-doubt than you give yourself credit for.

Maybe you showed up that one time to school, and you were self-doubting, but people liked you, and you were just fine. Perhaps that one time you went into that project, and you knew you didn't know how to do it, but by the end of that week, or the end of that month, you figured it out. You have to have a memory for the things you did overcome, as much as you worry about the things you lack. If your thought pattern is constantly repeating, "I lack, I lack, I lack, I lack, I lack..." of course you're going to self-doubt all the time, to a degree where you stop trying.

If you can have that positive self-talk and remind yourself of all the times, you overcame what you did not know, that will lead to genuine self-confidence.

You might find yourself saying: "You know what? I believe in my ability to figure things out. Even if I have some doubts about how it might go or doubts about how things might turn out, I know that I will figure it out. Give me enough time, energy, effort, resources, and support, and I can do it." As I said, that's genuine self-confidence. Even though you have doubts, the next time you're going into that situation where you have doubt, I want you to say, "You know what? I'll figure it out," and trust in that.

#2: Show up with intention.

If you want to deal with self-doubt, you absolutely must start entering each day with more intention. One of the reasons we don't believe in ourselves is because we're just all over the place.

Sometimes you're relaxed in this situation, but you're dumb in that situation. Sometimes you don't do well here, but you do well there. What happens is, so many people are going through the motions, or they're just showing up in life every single day, and they're reacting, and because they're constantly reacting, they don't have a character.

They haven't determined: Who am I? Who am I going to act like in this situation? Who am I going to behave like in this situation? How am I going to treat people in this situation? Because they haven't shown up with intention and sought to live out that intention, they feel a lot of discord in life. They don't know who they are because they just keep showing up and reacting to what's there. But guess what? What's there is always different.

The world is constantly changing, people are always changing, and situations are continually changing. If all you're ever doing is showing up and reacting, thinking, "I guess I'll just go through it and see how it goes," you're never forming an intentional character.

Of course, you doubt yourself because every situation is different, and you can never have certainty in that. But you can have the strength inside. From now on, wake up every day, and you say, "I'm going to be these three words today." And you just set the words, you say, "I'm going to be fun, I'm going to be playful, I'm going to be kind." And that day, you are fun, playful, and kind. And the next day, you say, "I'm going to be patient, thoughtful, and appreciative," and you act patient, thoughtful, and appreciative. You do that over and over and over again, set an intention for who you want to be, and be that.

Set an intention, and be that.

Do that in more situations in your life and more days, weeks, months, and years, and you'll be confident in yourself because you know that you can direct your mind, emotions, and body to be the person you want to be. The more often you do that, the more authentic, genuine self-confidence will come into your life.

#3: Get clarity, get a plan, get momentum.

You need to get clarity, you need to get a plan, and you need to gain momentum. Many people have self-doubt in their lives because they don't have clarity for what they want.

Many people wander into a situation, and they have a lot of self-doubts because they didn't sit down and plan it out. They didn't prepare. They didn't ask mentors or model others or do the research to figure out, "I should do a, b, c, d, and e." I can say, if you don't know the steps to success, of course, you'll have more self-doubt. If you don't have the plan, if you don't have the map, if you don't know what you're doing, of course, you're going to have more self-doubt.

Decide to build a plan, even if you have to ask for help.

Ask, "Hey, guys, how would you do this? What would be your first step? What would be your second step?" I'm always asking that. Even at this stage in my career, I'm still saying, "Hey guys, if you were going to launch this, how would you do it? If you were going to promote that, how would you do it? If you were going to create this thing, how would you do it? If you were going to build this team or build that business, what would you do?" I always try to get the map before I enter the woods so that I have the steps. I know the path because if you can remove the doubt about the course, you'll have more confidence in yourself.

#4: Learn vs. judge.

The fourth big idea for you (this one is so straightforward, but I think people don't do it) is that you need to learn versus judge when it comes to your behaviors and your results in life.

Start a Sunday review, and every Sunday, all I want you to do is sit down and evaluate how you showed up this last week. How did you show up, Monday, Tuesday, Wednesday, Thursday, and Friday?

What situations did you do well in? What conditions could you have done better in? What did you learn about yourself? And use that review session not to beat yourself up, or be mad at yourself, or to stir self-talk that's filled with self-hatred, but rather to say, "What did I learn about who I am, and what I prefer in life? What did I learn about what I like? What did I learn about the best of me, and what did I learn about the go-through-the-motions me? Where did I feel down? Where did I feel confident?"

Start experimenting with how you view yourself by doing a better job of reviewing your week.

People don't have as confident a mentality as they should because they're just barrelling through, oblivious to how much they've grown. Instead of judging yourself, you can have an entire self-evaluation session every week: How did I do, what did I learn? In that personal development, can you look at yourself objectively, without judging, without being mad, without giving it negative labels, and ask, "How did I do? What did I learn, what could I have done better?" Observe how you're going through your life, and then tell yourself, "Next time, I'll do this differently, and next time, I'll do this, and next time, I'll do that." That's a learning mentality versus a judgment mentality.

A judgment mentality is: I was an idiot. I was stupid. I didn't like myself. I look stupid. People are going to mock me; they're going to hate me. That judgmental self-talk leads to low self-confidence. Most people spend most of their time criticizing themselves. Their self-talk is negative instead of learning-oriented.

As soon as you switch from a negative standpoint to a learning standpoint, disappointment goes away, embarrassment goes away, self-hatred goes away, and you start just learning your way into the new and most vital you.

So next time you're plagued with self-doubt, think of a few of these things:

Reframe confidence, don't think you have to be completely confident. Just say, "You know what? I'm going to figure my way through this. It's going to be OK. I'm going to trust. I've figured out things in the past, and I'll figure out this one."

Make sure that you start each day or walk into each situation with a little more intention. Who do you want to be? And live into that more consistently because that will start to form the character you can take confidence in.

Make sure you get the plan; you take those steps, you get a little momentum because momentum comes with more confidence and a little more self-assuredness.

Make sure you are learning. Keep learning from me, keep learning from other people. Watch my other videos, listen to my podcast, read my books, listen to other people's podcasts and books. Get yourself in the game of personal development and into a perspective where you're learning about yourself, and you're proud of yourself for that growth.

Do you know when you're going to be the proudest of yourself? When you find real, genuine self-confidence and grow at the rate and the speed you genuinely desire. So keep learning, my friend, because listen: you're stronger than you think, and the future holds good things for you.

Made in the USA
Columbia, SC
28 April 2021